HUMAN
RESOURCES

KEEP UP THE
GOOD
WORK

But
FIRST
COFFEE

HUMAN
RESOURCES

DON’T MAKE
ME USE MY
HR
VOICE

But did you document it?

HR
QUEEN

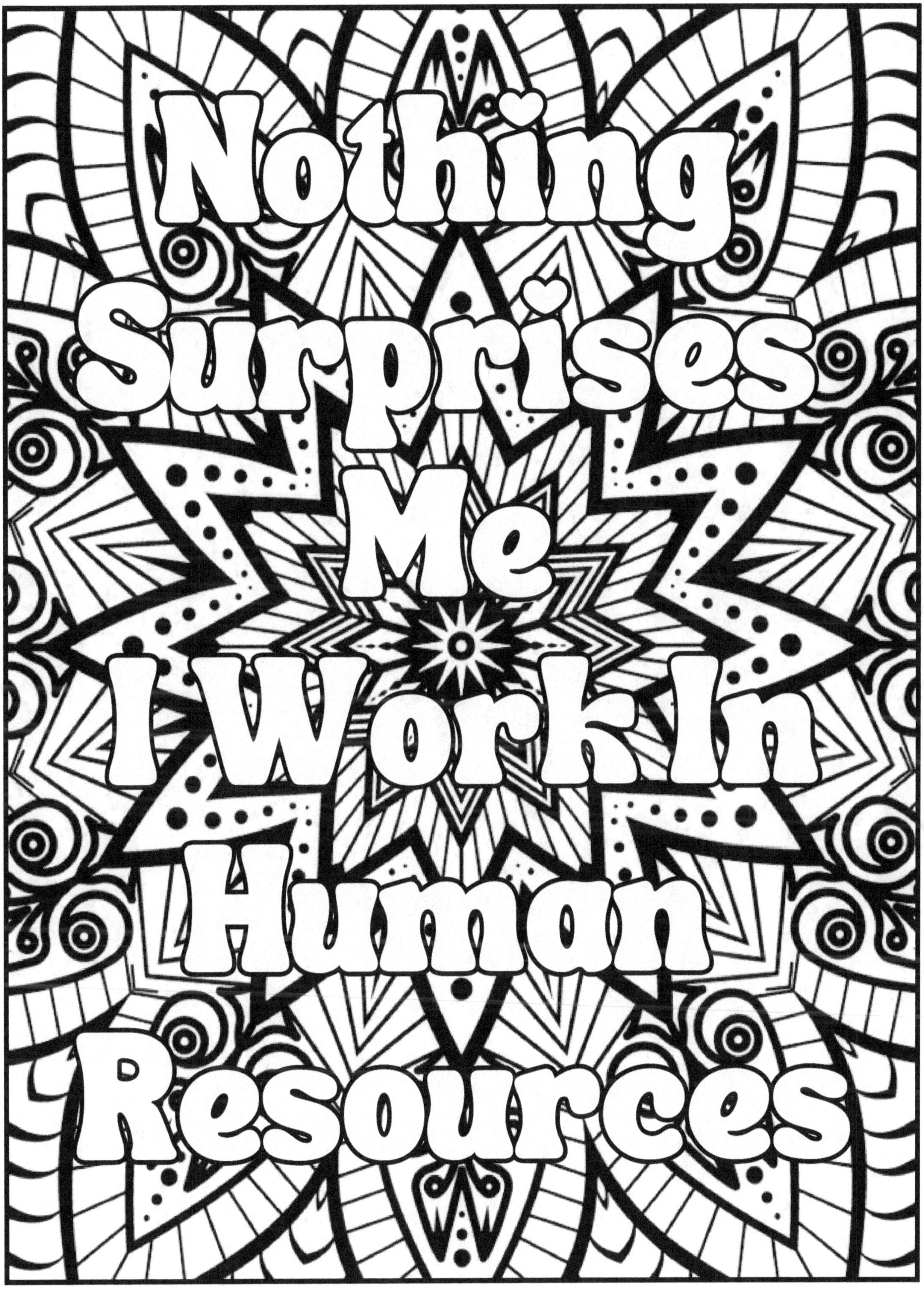
Nothing
Surprises
Me
I Work In
Human
Resources

What Happens In
HR
Stays in
HR

HIR

HR
SQUAD

YOU CAN'T
Spell
HERO
Without
"HR"

Live
what you
Love

Girl Boss

LIVE YOUR PURPOSE

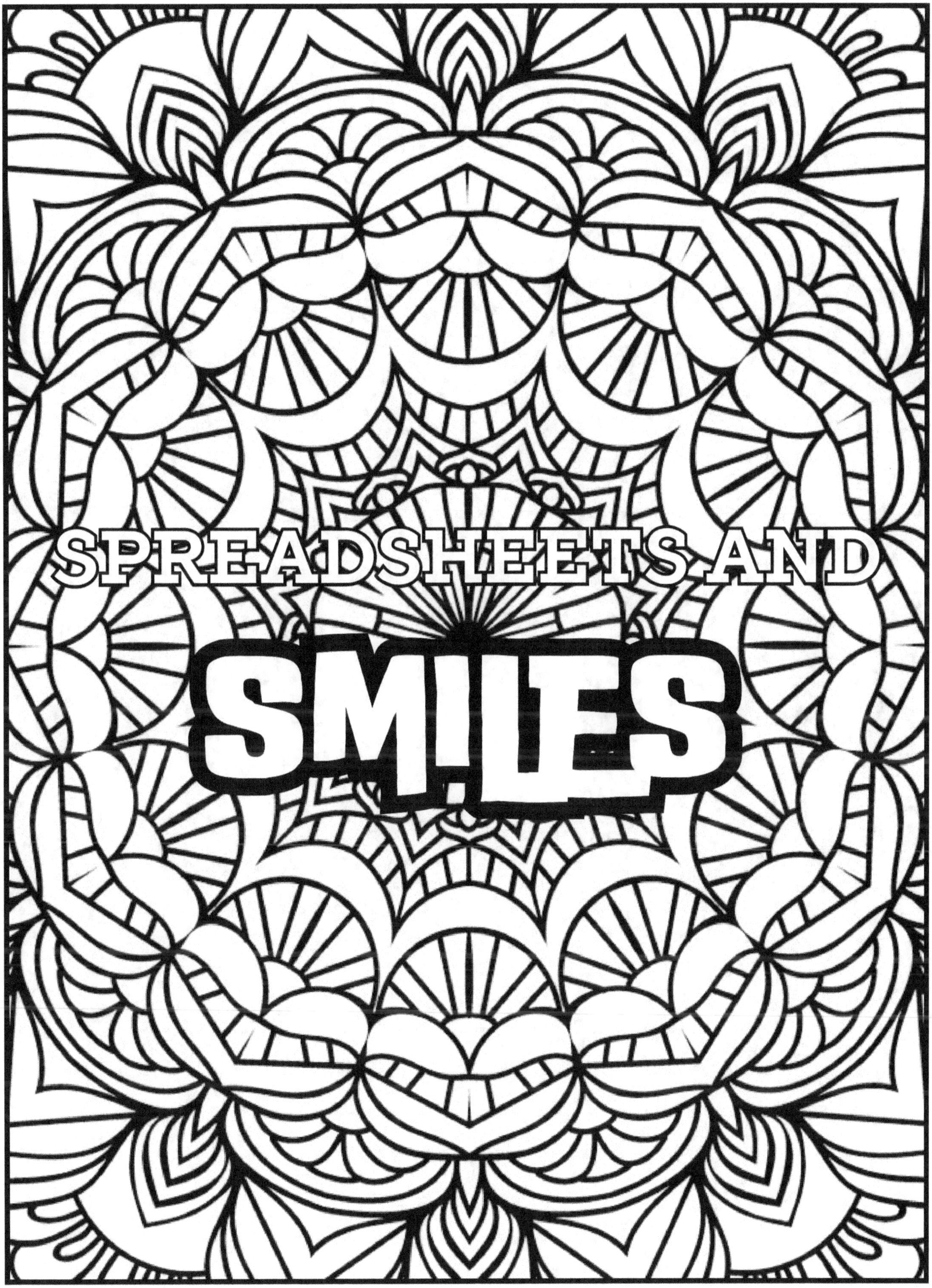
SPREADSHEETS AND
SMILES

LEADERSHIP
WHISPERER

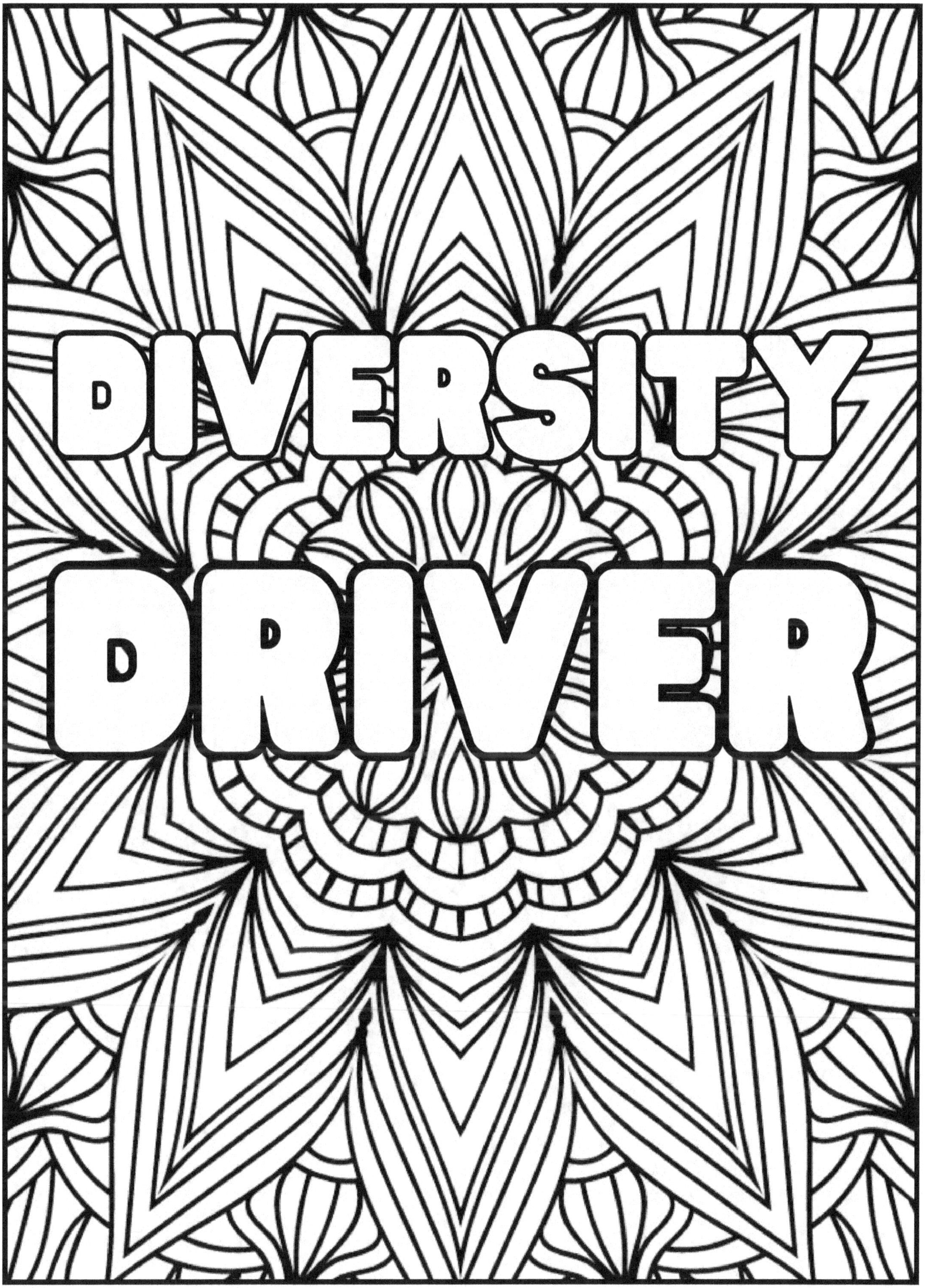
DIVERSITY
DRIVER

I can
&
I will

WAKE
UP &
SLAY

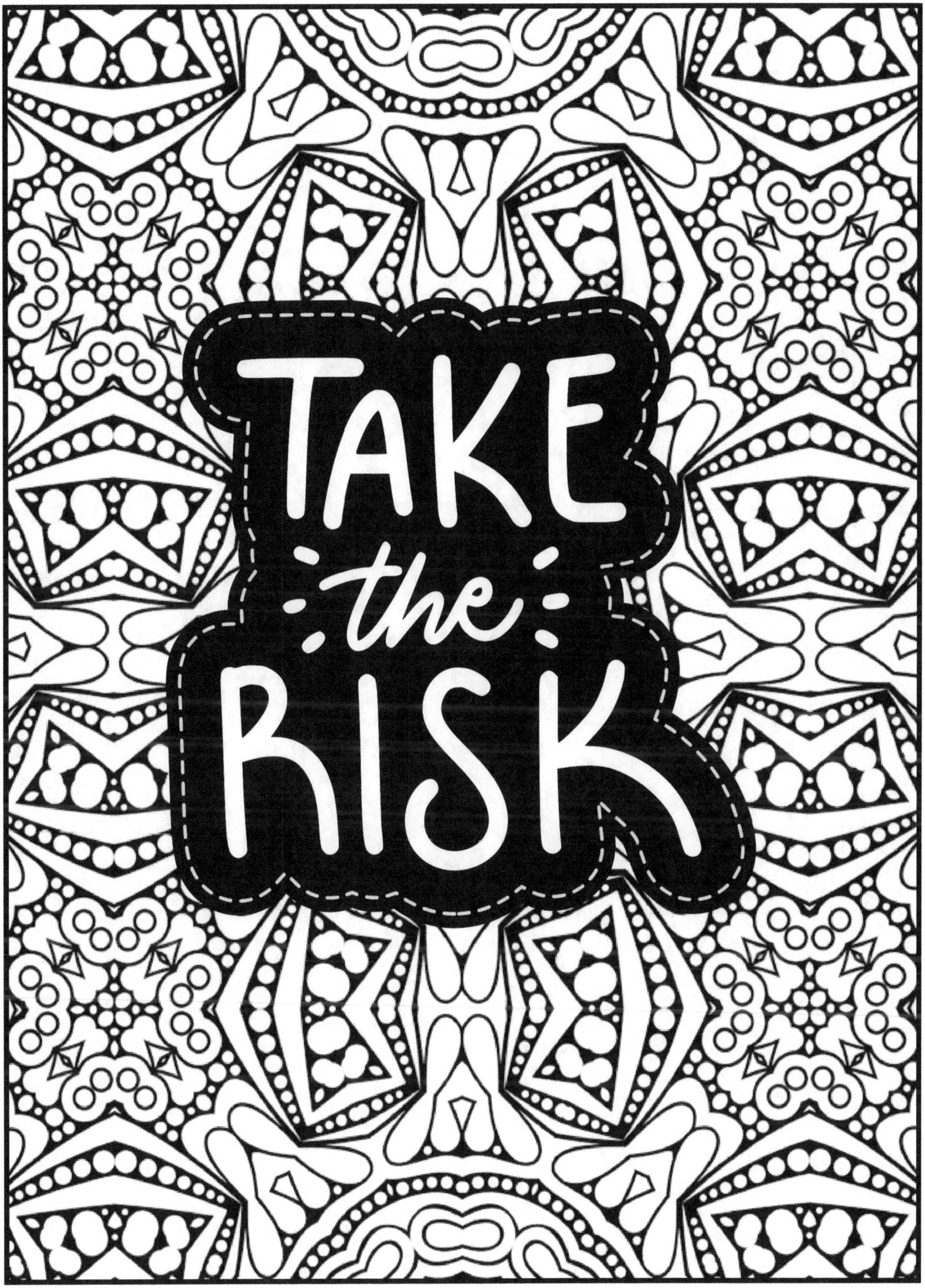
TAKE
the
RISK

IF YOU
WANT
APPLES
YOU HAVE TO
SHAKE THE
TREES

Just A
Girl
With
Goals

learn
SOMETHING
- new -
EVERYDAY

BE
Fearless

Be
GOOD
to
YOURSELF.

If you want it, work for it!

BE THE
BEST
VERSION
OF YOURSELF

Life
is full of
Possibilities

DON'T STOP
until
you're
PROUD

www.ingramcontent.com/pod-product-compliance
Lightning Source LLC
Chambersburg PA
CBHW082220220526
45470CB00010B/3241